C 19

*'the nineteenth century
murmured in our ears'*

C19

INTERTEXT || EKPHRASIS

Cassandra **ATHERTON**
Paul **HETHERINGTON**
Paul **MUNDEN**
Jen **WEBB**

authorised theft

C19: Intertext || Ekphrasis
authorised theft / Recent Work Press
Canberra, Australia

This chapbook series was produced with the support of the
International Poetry Studies Institute (IPSI), based within the
Centre for Creative and Cultural Research, Faculty of Arts and
Design, University of Canberra.
http://ipsi.org.au

Collection © Recent Work Press 2020
The copyright of the individual poems remains with the authors.
Design: Caren Florance

ISBN 978-0-6450090-4-0

Cover image: British Library digitised image from page 5 of
"Rona, a poem in seven books, illustrated with a ... map of
the Hebrides and ... engravings" https://www.flickr.com/
photos/britishlibrary/10997679114/

recentworkpress.com

Introduction: Intertextuality and Ekphrasis vii

Research Statement and Reflection:
Echoes of the 'Long 19th Century' x

Post-Raphaelite   Cassandra Atherton   1

The Novel Reader   Paul Hetherington   27

The Music Lovers   Paul Munden   51

The Persistence of Vision   Jen Webb   79

Individual poet statements   105

About the poets   118

The AUTHORISED THEFT series of poetry chapbooks was initiated by the International Poetry Studies Institute (IPSI) based in the Faculty of Arts and Design at the University of Canberra. The first collection of chapbooks—Cassandra Atherton's Pegs, *Paul Hetherington's* Jars, *Paul Munden's* Keys, *Jen Webb's* Gaps *and Jordan Williams'* Nets—*resulted from discussions connected to IPSI's Prose Poetry Project, inaugurated by IPSI in late 2014. A second collection,* The Taoist Elements, *followed in 2016; a third,* Colours, *in 2017; and a fourth,* Prosody, *in 2018. A fifth series,* The Six Senses, *followed in anthology form in 2019. This sixth collection builds on the same creative collaboration. IPSI supports and promotes collaborative and collegiate poetic work in a variety of forms, and encourages the collaboration of poets with other artists, such as Caren Florance who has designed the series.*

INTRODUCTION

Intertextuality and Ekphrasis
Paul Hetherington

This sixth collection of AUTHORISED THEFT chapbooks extends a collaborative project that has seen five poets conduct an extended exploration of the prose poetry form through writing on a variety of agreed ideas and themes. This year, for the first time there were four rather than five poets but the collaborative spirit continued unabated.

The 2020 series of chapbooks focuses on ways in which a conscious intertextuality and ekphrasis may be utilised in prose poetry to make connections between various forms of art in the 19th century and many of the preoccupations of contemporary life. In addressing this broad topic, each poet has chosen to focus on one of the following artistic domains: paintings/prints; music/songs; novels; and photography/film.

While Graham Allen reminds us that the term 'intertextuality' is complex and shifting—commenting that it 'is not a transparent term, and so ... cannot be invoked in an uncomplicated manner' (2000: 2)—nevertheless it is a useful concept for suggesting a variety of important ideas. These include Julia Kristeva's famous observation in 'Word, Dialogue and Novel' (1966) that 'any text is constructed as a mosaic of quotations; any text is the absorption and transformation of another. The notion of *intertextuality* replaces that of intersubjectivity, and poetic language is read as at least *double*' (1996: 37). Such a statement becomes especially interesting if we consider that 'texts' may, for example, be musical works or works of visual art, as well as literary works.

Kristeva's statement emphasises that all texts rely on and to a significant extent reiterate and interpret pre-existing texts and literary and cultural traditions, no matter how original a writer may believe they are, and that subtle webs of meaning, connection and influence permeate all reading. Roland Barthes extends this idea when he claims that 'the quotations a text is made of are anonymous, irrecoverable, and yet *already read*: they are quotations without quotation marks' (1989: 60).

In producing the works in these chapbooks, each poet has consciously exploited such ideas, drawing together meanings and associations that extend at least as far back as the 19th century and as far forward as 2020. The fact that 19th-century texts, images, films and objets d'art also, in turn, reach back toward even earlier texts and artefacts supports the idea that all art is created out of a process of interleaving and recycling; and that its innovations are based on previous expressions.

Ekphrasis, too, is complicated. James AW Heffernan comments that contemporary ekphrasis, as with earlier examples, primarily concerns itself with 'the conversion of fixed pose and gesture into narrative, the prosopopeial envoicing of the silent image, the sense of representational friction between signifying medium and subject signified' (2004: 136). Certainly, the prose poems in these chapbooks that deal with various forms of visual imagery engage with such conflicting ideas of representation and create a lively tension between 19th-century works and 21st-century ideas and perceptions.

Such ekphrastic prose poems are also, in a broad sense, intertextual, because all culture tends to move in and out of different forms of expression—so that a design that may have appeared, for example, in architecture may then find its way into a painting or sculpture, and before long have become a figuration in a work of literature. And, however one understands intertextuality—and even if one agrees that most intertextuality happens as a largely unconscious outcome of making creative work—a conscious intertextuality, along with the ekphrastic techniques mentioned, provides opportunities to explicitly acknowledge at least some of the debts that writers owe to those creative artists who have preceded them.

In this spirit I invite you to enjoy the *C19* chapbooks, that touch on the current pandemic as well as a previous century, and which, in doing so, create new and intriguing relationships and understandings.

Works Cited

Allen, G 2000 *Intertextuality*, London and New York: Routledge

Barthes, R 1989 *The Rustle of Language* (trans R Howard), Berkeley and Los Angeles, CA: University of California Press

Heffernan, JAW 2004 *Museum of Words: The Poetics of Ekphrasis from Homer to Ashbery*, Chicago, IL: The University of Chicago Press

Kristeva, J 1996 'Word, Dialogue and Novel', in T Moi (ed) *The Kristeva Reader: Julia Kristeva*, New York, NY: Columbia University Press, 34–61

RESEARCH STATEMENT & REFLECTION

Echoes of the 'Long 19th Century'
Jen Webb

In 2019, when we discussed the topic for this year's collection, we settled on a topic drawn from Paul Hetherington's poem 'Antiquities', which ends: 'Among our vernacular phrases, the nineteenth century murmured in our ears' (2018: 33). Back then, 'C19' referenced merely the '19th century', but as we began writing our poems on various forms of art from that period, and still as we complete this collection, C19 has become shorthand for the pandemic that has upended 2020, dominating the lives of pretty well everyone on the planet. Our starting point for this collection now feels uncomfortably prophetic, and it is tempting to draw a direct line between these two iterations of C19: each of them profoundly destructive, especially of people who are members of marginalised groups, and also profoundly generative—of science, philosophy, politics and, yes, art.

That frequently cited line—'The past is never dead. It's not even past' (Faulkner 1919: 85)—fits this context: to a significant extent we are still living under a type of 19th-century logic, and 'the principal dynamics' of the world remain 'defined predominantly by the downstream consequences of the 19th century' (Buzan & Lawson, 2015: 5). Historians regularly refer to that period as the 'long 19th century', calculating its range as 1776 to 1914 (see Hobsbawm 1989), because they detect a current of thought and progression of ideas that flowed across that period, and because, Karl Polayni writes, 'the civilization of the nineteenth century ... centred on a definite institutional mechanism' (1944: 4): a Eurocentric self-regulating economy, constant wrestling over the balance of power, military-imperialist adventurism and, above all, high finance.

These familiar pieces of the global jigsaw puzzle are still very much in play; and after all, although sound waves attenuate across time and space, they can take a long time to die, and the murmurings that Hetherington evokes in his poem remain, their products something of a curate's egg. Part of the impact includes the political and economic attitude that viewed the world and populations beyond Europe as mere raw material; and the resulting turbulence that led to the wars, mass movement of peoples, environment decay, and other disasters that characterise the 20th century. Another part is found in the thrilling energy that generated technical, scientific and philosophical developments, laid the foundations for the (tenuous but still extant) recognition that members of marginalised social groups have a claim on civil and political rights, and produced an efflorescence of art. This multilayered inheritance cannot be fully disentangled; the parts we might identify as negative contributed, in many ways, to the parts we claim as positive—and vice versa.

It is this latter we have focused on in our poetry: the paintings, photography, music and fiction that brought something very new into the world. In doing so, we do not look back with nostalgic gaze, but aim to produce an interweaving, or even a lamination, of the then and the now, recognising continuity in change. Elizabeth Grosz observes that 'philosophy functions like a kind of art and art as a kind of philosophy' (McDonald, Grosz & Rothfield 2006: 8), and in these sets of poems, each of us operates as artist (crafting something new out of what has come before) and as philosopher (asking, and finding answers to, questions about past and present, authorship and ownership, difference and representation). Nor do we ignore the 'great transformation' that Polanyi critiques, recognising that where the first C19 leads to rapacious imperialism and unchecked economic expansion, the second C19 is the bill that has to be paid for that attitude and all it generated. We work, through ekphrasis and inflection, with what we find in the thinking and outputs of 19th-century artists, hoping to contribute to the patterns of thinking, emotional landscapes and new modes of exchange that might be directed toward a kind of recovery.

Works Cited

Buzan, B and Lawson G 2015 *The Global Transformation: History, Modernity and the Making of International Relations*, Cambridge: Cambridge University Press

Faulkner, W 1919 *Requiem for a Nun*, London: Chatto & Windus

Hetherington, P 2018 *Moonlight on Oleander: Prose Poems*, Crawley: UWA Publishing

Hobsbawm, E 1989 *The Age of Empire: 1875–1914*, London: Weidenfeld & Nicolson

McDonald, H, Grosz, E and Rothfield, P 2006 'Art and Deleuze: A round table interview with Elizabeth Grosz', *Australian and New Zealand Journal of Art* 7 (2), 4–22

Polanyi, K 1944 *The Great Transformation: The Political and Economic Origins of our Time*, Boston, MA: Beacon Press

Post-Raphaelite

CASSANDRA ATHERTON

'Her hair that lay along her back was yellow like ripe corn.'
—*Dante Gabriel Rossetti*

'Low sit I down at my Lady's feet / Gazing through her wild eyes, / Smiling to think how my love will fleet / When their starlike beauty dies.'
—*Elizabeth Siddall*

Notice in the press and on social media	5
Beata Beatrix	6
Veronica Veronese	7
La Belle Iseult	8
A Sea Spell	9
The Beguiling of Merlin	10
Roman Widow	11
La Belle Dame Sans Merci	12
Proserpine	13
The Blue Bower	14
Lady Lilith	15
Circe Invidiosa	16
Love Among the Ruins	17
The Lady of Shalott	18
The Bridesmaid	19
Awakening Conscience	20
Isabella	21
Regina Cordium	22
The Magic Circle	23
Arthur's Tomb	24
Ophelia	25
Self-Portrait in Oil: Elizabeth Siddall	26

Notice in the press and on social media

As the *Love, Sex & Death* Pre-Raphaelite exhibition is unable to travel to the National Gallery of Victoria due to COVID-19, the Pre-Raphaelite paintings will be posted on Instagram weekly. Melbournians are invited to post their ekphrastic poems in the comments. Post-pandemic, one poem for each painting will be printed on the back of exhibition postcards, which will be available to purchase in our online giftshop.

Beata Beatrix (c. 1864–1870)

If you elegise me, do it slowly. Don't write a pantoum one evening over a chicken curry. Or a villanelle on the train between suburban stations. Take your time, compose a prose poem longhand in a notebook with a fountain pen. Buy an inkwell and fill it with pink ink. Let it stain your writing fingers. Set aside a few nights each month to put in commas and take out adjectives. Picture me in every metonym and alliteration; imagine us inhabiting the spaces between words. When it's finished, don't publish it. Make a bonfire and watch the paper catch and burn—the letters taking off like hundreds of fireflies in the starless night.

Veronica Veronese (1872)

Long days dreaming of a luthier's hands on her ribs, back and belly. Gentle, prolonged touch, he would take his time with the purfling. Late in the afternoon, she'd draw the green velvet curtains and he'd call her his red-hued beauty. She imagines vibrating under his expert fingers as his hands trace the curve of her ribs. He'd leave the smell of linseed oil and Venetian turpentine in her bed, a treble timbre between her sheets. Hoping for an encore, she'd spend the evening trying to recapture his music on the soft spruce of her belly.

for PM

La Belle Iseult (1858)

In dark rooms, with slow rhythms, you unmake me. You lie me sideways across the bed. Arched backs, like conjoined parentheses, skin on skin—a blissful roiling and churning. Afterwards, I hold you in a complicated desire to slow the separation of flesh and breath. In a few hours you will travel back across the border, leaving behind our tangled sheets as an unfinished portrait of what we made.

A Sea Spell (1877)

We share a triangular hotel room during stage three lockdown. Champagne bottles line the kitchen wall and every evening before bed I pull on your t-shirt and sneak down the corridor to put oyster shells and fish bones down the rubbish chute. I wedge the door open with my notebook. At night, we hook my computer to the television and watch old movies. You tell me I look like Glynis Johns in *Miranda* and I revel in crimpy hair and, at breakfast, sardines on toast. For ten days, the bed is our ocean. On the last morning, as we walk along the beach, I throw my half-eaten danish to a waiting seagull.

The Beguiling of Merlin (1872–1877)

In the serviced apartment, his leg presses against mine from hip to ankle. When I don't shift, I can feel the edges of his hesitation curl into a question mark. I read from his book, trace the curves of words like they are braille and speak them back to him. There are no constellations on his cheek, just danger in his touch. At the arboretum, we share an egg and avocado panini. Under a flowering Cockspur hawthorn he says he'd forgotten what it was like to laugh.

Roman Widow (1874)

He texts me ten-year-old photos from our Roman holiday; vivid missives from the time we walked uneven laneways and patted lazy cats' bellies in the *Cimitero dei protestanti*. By Shelley's heartless ashes, I traced the words *Cor Cordium* as a ginger feline reclined at my feet. I remember him telling me half of Thomas Hardy's heart was eaten by a cat and I laughed, thinking it preferable to encasement in a silver memorial. 'I'd elegise your fingers,' I said, 'or a little part of your frontal lobe'. He asked why I wouldn't wear his heart in a silken shroud around my neck.

La Belle Dame Sans Merci (1893)

When I leave, you call me *La Belle Dame Sans Merci*, keep my purple underwear for an empty ransom and breathe in my perfume from the pillowcase. For months, you play break-up songs while eating crumpets with honey in the mornings and roasting sweet potatoes in the afternoon. Your friends say you should always be suspicious of barefooted women. After long nights with my lasso of red hair haunting your neck, you say you'll spend eternity imagining the sound of other men surrendering on my sheets.

Proserpine (1874)

There is freedom in Summer, in blue heaven Slurpees and al fresco dining. My lover throws the sheet from his body and the sun stripes his legs like bright stockings. Sometimes we open the window and the breeze is jasmine in the morning, burning citronella candles in the evening. One time he suggested we go to Bath in June to prolong our season; drink champagne with chilli mussels and look out over rooftops from an apartment with a turquoise door. But I promised to spend winter with someone else, drinking hot chocolate with marshmallows, burrowing beneath the king-size doona. When blossom starts to creep across branches, a book arrives in the mail with six pomegranate seeds pressed between the pages.

The Blue Bower (1865)

At Hotel Granvia, a skinny Santa Claus in a blue fur suit rings a bell to announce the roast beef is being carved. You take up a naked plate while I wait for the cheesy happiness at the bottom of a seafood doria. I'm post-martini and you've had three glasses of wine. Salarymen fuelled by bottomless *tokkuri* of *saké* are cheering as the Christmas tree casts a pattern of turquoise light over the buffet. You nudge a silver orgel, from the Imperial Palace, across the table. When I open the lid, it plays *Happy Birthday* and blue Santa brings me a slice of strawberry shortcake on a heart-shaped plate. I take the cherry blossom from inside the music box and one of its tiny petals comes to rest beside my dessert spoon; a pink dot like a full stop.

Lady Lilith (1866–1873)

He rings to tell me I left an apple core in the small green bin in his bathroom. Red Delicious, with the seeds exposed around its narrow middle, his wife found it three days after I'd gone, decomposing in furry strips and mottled dots on the white flesh. I don't remember apples or offscourings, just kisses on my bare shoulder as I pulled long, orange hairs from my brush each morning, winding them into bright loops. Now I think of the hair nesting at the bottom of the bin liner, stuck to a rotting apple.

Circe Invidiosa (1892)

Early mornings, I run to the *Dogana da Mar* to stand on the triangle's tip, surrounded on three sides by all that blue. I tried calling, to show you the point where the Grand Canal meets the Giudecca Canal, but you were tucked up in a different time zone. In the apartment in San Marco, a previous lover makes me peanut butter and strawberry jam on rye, a relic of breakfasts years ago. But I prefer waiting for lunches of crisp prosecco and tramezzini at *Enoteca al Volto*. Standing as if on the prow of a boat, I imagine my water bottle becoming an ombra of wine and, as the sun weakens, I toast the shadows lengthening on the water's surface.

Love Among the Ruins (1894)

At Madrid–Barajas Airport I wandered between the hanging jamón and a rack of turquoise dresses at *Zara*. Passport between my lips, I pulled the lace hem over my head, trying it on over my clothes. 'You should get it,' you said. But my hand luggage was already weighed down with a tin of smoked paprika, a tiny snow globe and a flamenco tumbler. When *Burberry* didn't have the jeans you wanted, the sales assistant offered you alternatives. I tucked your boarding pass into my passport and re-zipped the jeans you discarded. You walked around the store in Straight Fit Washed Denim and the sales assistant asked, 'What does your wife think?' In the long silence, I realised twilight at the *Thyssen* was our last blue hour and when you raised an eyebrow at me I said, 'Yes, you should get them.'

The Lady of Shalott (1888)

In the late afternoon, my cat stretches out on the boat's deck and I pat his belly in the low hanging sunlight. There's a salty sweet smell of silver waves as our floating house sways in the gathering wind. Later, when it gets colder, I'll take the patchwork quilt from my bed and we'll listen to the rhythm of carp banging their tails on the hull.

for PH

The Bridesmaid (1851)

On their first wedding anniversary, she messages me to say she ate the top layer of their three-tiered wedding cake for breakfast, washing down the marzipan and dark fruit cake with honey and peppermint tea. I take my slice out of the fridge, still preserved in its *Thank you* paper bag and see my lover's teeth marks in the royal icing. 'You prefer croquembouche, anyway,' he says, pushing his fingers through the cross-sections of my orange braid. He follows me into the bedroom and I tuck the paper bag of cake under my pillow. 'Your hair is like poetry,' he says. 'A sonnet?' I ask. 'Epic,' he insists, lifting a crimpy strand to his nose. It's corny but makes me smile. As he rakes his fingers through my kinks, I start to unravel.

Awakening Conscience (1853)

Your wife tells me my hair reminds her of the woman in Hunt's oil on canvas, and we both know which painting she means. It's not really about my orange hair—she thinks I'm the kind of woman who sits on men's laps. So I tell her, 'Once I sat on a Pulitzer prize judge's lap at a book launch. He asked me to stay with him in London, but his wife retracted the invitation.' Your wife nods. 'I think my lap sitting started with Santa Claus; I've just never really shaken the habit.' Walking over to the window, I want to tell you how on my first flight over I thought an extreme patch of turbulence was a biblical intervention to protect your lap from my buttocks. But when I safely landed, I realised it was not a *deux ex machina* but an anti-climax.

Isabella (1848–1849)

Small talk on a long table. She smiles at the rhythmic clanking of bottles on the rims of sturdy wine glasses. She's on the periphery of chatter, a dreamy lethargy in her limbs. As the hotel cat jumps into her lap, she knocks over the salt-shaker and throws a pinch over her left shoulder. Someone says, 'Don't look back'. He pulls up a chair to sit beside her; conversation follows him. Offering her translucent segments of blood orange from his plate, his fingers cast distorted shadows on the tablecloth. She remembers the first time he touched her spine; his outline pressed into her sheets. They are all watching as he dips a piece of orange in her wine. He leaves first, taking the lift to his room. She follows ten minutes later, taking the stairs.

Regina Cordium (1860)

Our love is a study in pink and red; a rush of hearts and kisses. In front of the shiny red doors of the Old South Meeting House, we overwrite *til death do us part*, with *forever*. My neck warms my grandmother's beads as you slide your hands beneath my veil and kiss me. The sounding board over the pulpit is our red-cushioned witness.

for Bay

The Magic Circle (1886)

She bewitches him slowly with her sous chef and *mise en place* skills. The first time, she roughly chops the whole head of garlic for their pasta sauce. Severing the top and tail of each clove, she enjoys the slow press of each one between the flat knife blade and chopping board. She denudes them, sliding off their paper skins, and feels the fragrant stickiness on her fingers. The next time, she slices a habanero in thin strips and encourages him to eat the leftover seeds while the shakshuka is baking. After that, she becomes the official grater of Grana Padano; the triangular wedge of cheese slowly becoming a rectangle in her fingers. They buy a pan at his local store and cook scallop risotto under a sickle moon; the hot scent of butter and mollusc rising in a lemon haze. Her arms around him are an ouroboros as she leads him deeper into the garden.

Arthur's Tomb (1860)

1. Halfway between sleep and wakefulness he puts his hand over hers. On their honeymoon she told him she hoped they'd die in exactly the same moment, as if they shared the same heart. When she stretches her fingers, his pinky rests in the crook of her thumb. She holds it there.

2. She listens to *Avalon* on her lover's couch while they drink champagne. As he refills her glass he says, 'You can love more than one person at the same time.' She looks down at the champagne flute resting between her finger and thumb.

Ophelia (1851–1852)

I wade into the lake, hitching the red ballgown around my waist; white legs disappearing in inches. The photographer is in waterproof waders, clearing the water with a leaf catcher. As I stretch out mermaid-like, she drapes the organza skirt across the water's surface and places a book on my chest. I lie between lily pads, white-tipped pink waterlilies framing my face. As I float, the water tugs at the hem of my dress and the long train starts to sink, winding itself around my knees. I think of Lizzie in the bath, heavy white dress, nostrils just above the water line.

for Donna Squire

Elizabeth Siddal:
Self Portrait in Oil (1854)

A nine-inch green circle; Lizzie through her own grey eyes. I want to tell you that I am my own muse; I don't need to mythologise our moments as golden vignettes or blue fragments. But it's easier to be Ophelia, Guggums or Blanchefleur. I look for my voice but find myself visiting Tate Britain when I'm in London. I hide behind heartsease, daffodils and white roses. I leave a lantern on her grave at Highgate. On the old stone I can still make out the words: To the memory of Elizabeth Eleanor.

The Novel Reader

PAUL HETHERINGTON

'Literature simulates life. A novel is a story of what never was.'
—*Fernando Pessoa*

'Some books leave us free and some books make us free.'
—*Ralph Waldo Emerson*

1.

We occupy my sister-in-law's second apartment, living in cramped quarters with my husband's anger at being sacked. My own working hours have been halved; the house we'd hoped to renovate is on the market. I inhabit the congestion of nineteenth-century novels. *Haggard anxiety and remorse are bad companions to be barred up with.* We drink wine and mull over eight years of marriage. 'Nothing,' I say, 'prepared me for being trapped.' Reading becomes a prophecy of days: *a burning restlessness sets in, an agonised impatience.*

2.

He shouts and hurls a pretty cup, leaving me to collect the pieces. *When I appear before him now, he has no such honeyed terms as 'love' and 'darling'.* Mostly, I dwell in others' language—locating wider reaches; salving and saving myself; stepping onto nameless shores—through distances of paragraphs. I climb into carriages; board rickety vessels; clamber over moors and white roads, *behind and on each hand of me ... and the heather grows deep and wild to their very verge.*

3.

I'm sick and he barely speaks to me, though twice he leaves a bowl of soup with bits of vegetable floating in it. My thoughts are dark as inked cotton, as if my mind is smeared—and *the usual tenor of my life becomes like an old remembrance*—distanced from everything I once believed. Eventually he calls a doctor who diagnoses my state of mind as a symptom of the flu. He prescribes pills but *I seem to have crossed a dark lake and to have left all my experiences, mingled together by the great distance, on the healthy shore.*

4.

I begin to crave the sea, though I haven't been on a boat for ten years. Before I met him, I'd travelled to Tristan da Cunha. Isolation was my dream—a small community and self-sufficiency. I stayed and thought of marrying there. But the south Atlantic wind blew up, the volcano stirred and the ocean pummelled its rocks. I remembered *in landlessness alone resides highest truth*; thought of the *cold malicious waves*—and, despite this, could not stay. Now, in this apartment, my wish for self-sufficiency returns—we're almost ruined by closing walls. Is it better, after all, *to perish in that howling infinite, than be ingloriously dashed upon the lee, even if that were safety*? My husband prowls like a captain.

5.

He's in bed, blaming me for his sickness. I let him sleep. For days I bask in words and antiquarian worlds. I'm the heroine of a hundred, indelible moments: *She would have liked to live in some old manor-house, like those long-waisted chatelaines who, in the shade of pointed arches, spent their days leaning on the stone, chin in hand, watching a cavalier.* I hate the modern world and its exigencies, and while it's absurd to imagine the chatelaine's life as ideal ... my husband calls from the bedroom, coughing and swearing.

6.

He's worse than before, still wheezing and refusing Benadryl. I open the window, letting new air feed the white camellias in the vase. I watch the traffic and see a young man stepping onto the road—a neighbour's boy. Cars brake and judder; he stands unmoved until a siren splits the morning. On television, politicians argue over borders. *Such people there are living and flourishing in the world—Faithless, Hopeless, Charityless.* I dream of travelling worlds away; searching old language for directions as cures are predicted around the globe: *Some there are, and very successful too, mere quacks and fools ...*

7.

Is it strange to be in love one minute and, a few minutes later, not? For eight years I would have declared my love, but there was a moment—it seemed almost instantaneous. I would hardly have believed it—to feel so changed. I look toward the back garden and it represents a way out; I hear my husband dressing and have no desire to see him. *I am taken with an impulse that might master me, I feel, completely should I give it the least encouragement ...*

8.

Knowing someone; not knowing them—as if marriage is unconvincing fiction. Having immersed myself in it, I'm not sure what I understood. I read hungrily, looking for truths—many like accusations: *She had thought she knew her husband so well, was amazed at his appearance when he went in to her. His brow was lowering, and his eyes stared darkly* ... I took his hands, pressing them to my body—so often we'd done this, finding a way. Although warm, his body felt like a dead man's, we had so little connection. He pulled away; I leaned against the wall as he yelled that he'd stepped on a porcelain splinter from the thrown cup: 'What's wrong with you?' Then he was silent—*his mouth was tightly and contemptuously shut.*

9.

Insomniac, I slide from the sheets, listening to his breathing. Even in bed, there are oceans of distance between us. But I wonder what separation means in a two-room apartment. Soon, I'm in front of the long mirror, pushing threads of hair from my face. *Her figure looks singularly tall and imposing as she stands in her long white nightgown.* I become nervous he'll wake and come to find me; that he'll grab me by my hair ... *hanging like pot-hooks.*

10.

I wake, thinking of a dream. I'd been standing on tiptoe in the rain, peering into a house through a window. The room contained a chandelier and the house was lavishly furnished, with a sense of charged light. After a while, two figures entered— my husband and I—in an argument. I saw myself pick up a large candelabra from a sideboard and strike him with it. There was blood on my right hand. Despite this, as rain soaked me, I kept thinking how beautiful the house was and how I wanted to be inside—*a splendid place carpeted with crimson, and crimson-covered chairs and tables, and a pure white ceiling bordered by gold, a shower of glass-drops hanging in silver chains from the centre ...*

11.

My husband begins to talk affectionately, but I tell him, 'Never again'. We don't speak for days. It's a form of agony but we have no easy way to end it. Our rooms are tight, as if emotions obstruct our movement. I stay in the bedroom, a novel on my lap: *She sits in her corner, so motionless, so passive, simply with the sense of being carried ... she recalls to herself one of those Etruscan figures couched upon the receptacle of their ashes.* I see myself in a mirror, dark-eyed, barely understanding the image carries my name. I begin to think of myself as a marionette but can't imagine anyone holding the slumping strings.

12.

He takes a book from my hands and drops it in the kitchen bin. An action movie begins on the television and the room fills with shouts and images of men on a ski slope. One falls from a high cliff. I rescue the book and brush food scraps from its cover. I consider *chatterers who attempt only the smallest achievements, being indeed equipped for no other.* Cold gathers the room and on the television screen a man slides across ice toward me. My husband receives a text message and reminds me we agreed to meet friends at a café, now that restrictions have been eased. *To have reversed a previous arrangement and declined to go out would have been a show of persistent anger.* He removes the book from my hands again. I pull on shoes and push hair from my face as a dense snowfall begins.

13.

We attempt a rapprochement. I push words I don't believe into the apartment, my mouth speaking as if with a ventriloquist's voice. I can't say 'love' but find sufficient words to draw him toward me. His hands cradle my face and he manoeuvres me into the bedroom—yet I might be a sculpture; a plundered statue from Corinth, piled into a ship's hold. I try to recollect the tenderness of hands that shaped and moulded feeling like clay. But everything seems belated—as if I no longer live in the present tense, and *all my past life was now a blot, a blind vacancy in which I distinguish nothing.*

14.

He talks of travelling, remembering the narrow streets of Barrio Gótico; of crowded Las Ramblas; of a bar where we got drunk. I nod as the edge of my best friend's letter, hidden inside my underwear, irritates my thigh. It evokes our trip to Venice when we were nineteen: 'Can you picture us, even now, *floating down the green water-ways of the pink and pearl city, seated in a black gondola with silver prow and trailing curtains?*' We were beguiled by the streets of water and rotting architecture, walking hand-in-hand, speaking of women's hidden lives.

15.

In becoming a stranger to my husband, I realise I've been seeing him as if through a bright gauze curtain. I slice a lemon and run my tongue across the flesh. It tingles—such sourness was a childish pleasure, my mother handing me lemon slices as she cooked: 'It's a mystery that you like them.' I reached for her floury hands as she kneaded dough but didn't fathom her sense of being apart. 'Women must choose,' she told me, 'between their life or a life lived for others.' I look at the neighbouring windows, *reflecting that every one of those darkly clustered houses encloses its own secret.*

16.

My mother owned what she called an Indian cabinet. When I was a child, I thought it exotic. She kept odds and ends in it, as well as stationery, and an unset emerald that she'd 'found' as a young woman. 'It's Colombian,' she said on one of the few occasions I saw her handle it. More than once, my father suggested she have it set into a ring. In my late teens, poking around underneath the cabinet, I found it to be *full of queer drawers, little pigeonholes, and secret places, in which were kept all sorts of ornaments, some precious, some merely curious.* A concealed drawer sprang open containing a bundle of letters from 'Your Tom'. Reading them I felt outrage—and unexpected pleasure. My mother's lover had given her the 'green and lovely stone'.

17.

I think of my mother and distant father. I think of my husband's comment, 'You're worthless'. I'd refused to let him touch me and his anger still fills the apartment like a flood. I hear *faintly ... a sound like bells or like a band* and, after he falls asleep, I slip out and follow an alley to the local bar, finding myself among a crowd. Lights dim and the music swells. A man reaches over and grabs me, saying 'Come here, sweet girl'. *On this whole scene was impressed a dream-like character: every shape was wavering, every movement floating, every voice echo-like—half-mocking, half-uncertain.*

18.

I disentangle myself and return home, sliding into bed. Next morning, my husband turns on the television after breakfast. I stand in front of the bathroom mirror again, wondering how others see me. I begin to undress, trying to imagine myself as a man watching a lover, how he might have once watched me: *she loosened her clothes, removing the greater part of them. She bathed her face, her neck and arms in the basin that stood between the windows. She took off her shoes and stockings and stretched herself.* I remember how we used to lie together, playing with each other. I shut the bedroom door and begin to read.

19.

A second letter arrives. My best friend suggests we meet as soon as possible. She conjures Venice on warm, seductive evenings and concerts we attended. Her words give new piquancy to the observation: *Why is it that when one is enjoying, say, a piece of music, or a beautiful summer evening, or a conversation with a sympathetic companion, the occasion seems rather a hint at an infinite felicity existent elsewhere than a real felicity actually being experienced?* She recalls the violinist in a church performance of Vivaldi's *The Four Seasons*. He was so immersed in the music that its progress could be read in the changing expressions on his face—we sat close to the front and were engrossed.

20.

I'm afraid I'll exchange one difficult relationship for another. My affection for my husband lingers—but at one remove, as if my feelings are no longer grounded. He senses the change and complains less. I waver, thinking of our last eight years, and he buys me a necklace of lapis lazuli. *Nor were it an inconsistency too improbable to be assigned to human nature, should we suppose a feeling of regret ... at the moment when she was about to win her freedom.*

21.

Days stretch and my best friend writes of the future as if it's already coming to pass. The trouble I have in leaving hardly occurs to her. We talk on the phone and there's something unsettling that repels even as it attracts. Perhaps, after all, I'll patch my marriage up—though he continues to shout. *I hold that I have a right to sadness and stillness; I nurse them for their postponing power*—worrying that there are no good choices. My books sustain me still.

Notes to the Prose Poems

Italicised passages in the prose poems have been taken from the following books, with the only amendments being their recontextualisation, along with occasional changes of tense to match that of the prose poems in which they appear: 1: Charles Dickens, *Little Dorrit*; 2: Charlotte Brontë, *Jane Eyre*; 3: Charles Dickens, *Bleak House*; 4: Herman Melville, *Moby-Dick*; 5: Gustave Flaubert, *Madame Bovary*; 6: William Makepeace Thackeray, *Vanity Fair*; 7: Henry James, *The Turn of the Screw*; 8: Leo Tolstoy, *Anna Karenina*; 9: Thomas Hardy, *Tess of the d'Urbervilles*; 10: Emily Brontë, *Wuthering Heights*; 11: Henry James, *The Portrait of a Lady*; 12: George Eliot, *Middlemarch*; 13: Mary Shelley, *Frankenstein*; 14: Oscar Wilde, *The Picture of Dorian Gray*; 15: Charles Dickens, *A Tale of Two Cities*; 16: Louisa May Alcott, *Little Women*; 17: Charlotte Brontë, *Villette*; 18: Kate Chopin, *The Awakening*; 19: Ivan Turgenev, *Fathers and Sons*; 20: Nathaniel Hawthorne, *The Scarlet Letter*; 21: Henry James, *The Wings of the Dove*.

The Music Lovers

PAUL MUNDEN

'Deep inside us all there is something that speaks to us and drives us, almost unconsciously, and that may emerge at times sounding as poetry or music.'
—*Johannes Brahms*

'Do yourself a favor and go find the originals.'
—*Guns n' Roses*

Ludwig van Beethoven, *Sinfonia Eroica*	55
Hector Berlioz, *Symphonie Fantastique*	56
Niccolò Paganini, *Moto Perpetuo*	57
Frédéric Chopin, Prelude No. 15, 'Raindrop'	58
Clara Schumann, Konzertsatz	59
Modest Mussorgsky, *Pictures at an Exhibition*	60
Richard Wagner, *Götterdämmerung*	61
Arthur Sullivan, 'The Lost Chord'	62
Bedřich Smetana, String Quartet No. 1, 'From My Life'	63
Charles-Marie Widor, Toccata, from Symphony for Organ No. 5	64
Camille Saint-Saëns, 'Kangaroos', from *The Carnival of the Animals*	65
Claude Debussy, *Claire de lune*	66
Engelbert Humperdink, *Hänsel und Gretel*	67
Antonín Dvořák, Symphony No. 9, 'From the New World'	68
Richard Strauss, *Also Sprach Zarathustra*	69
Edward Elgar, Variations on an Original Theme, 'Enigma'	70
Maurice Ravel, *Pavane pour une infante défunte*	71
Jean Sibelius, *Finlandia*	72
Sergei Rachmaninoff, Piano Concerto No. 2	73
Alma Mahler, 'Einsamer Gang'	74
William Harris, 'Bring Us, O Lord God'	76

Ludwig van Beethoven,
Sinfonia Eroica *(1803)*

When you hear that Bonaparte has appointed himself Emperor, you lose your rag, crossing out the dedication with such fury you scuff a hole in the page
                          before   tearing it up, for good measure. Then you get ahead of yourself too, at bar 394, the horn announcing the main theme's return, two bars early, clashing with the strings. Haydn is speechless, head in hands; even Berlioz thinks you've lost it, ffs, but you're deaf to the critique. Later, overwhelmed by a torrent of silence, you beat the keyboard senseless, so that listeners struggle to hear any order in the jangling cacophony. Slowly, over the course of the next two hundred years, our hearing comes back. *I'd give this piece four stars. Stumbled on the YouTube film, thinking it said Erotica, but hey—not bad!*

Eroica, dir. Cellan Jones, 2003

Hector Berlioz, Symphonie Fantastique:
Épisode de la vie d'un artiste ...
en cinq parties *(1830)*

He's in the theatre that night, as Hamlet lifts poor Yorick's skull, travelling through time. It could be David Tennant, holding Tchaikovsky's remains like a glass of water to the light; it could be anyone; it doesn't matter; Hector only has eyes for Harriet Smithson as Ophelia, instantly obsessed. When she fails to reply to his letters, he assembles a team of crack musicians, clad in black. They play by heart, the artist's unrequited passion—his delirium—seared into their brains. And so it erupts, symphony as story; the woman who ignores him the *idée fixe* within the soundtrack of his life.

And we're with him all the way—the delusional lord of the dance—as he drags us down, deeper and down ...

There's a moment of calm, a day when the *ranz des vaches* is calling to me across an alpine meadow from the past, with dark questions that I can't answer.

The music grows feverish, murderous in its dreams. It's a trip to hell. *Long aerial tracking shot of a yellow beetle travelling through the mountains to the Overlook Hotel.*

And now the musicians don white paper masks like skeletal, antlered beasts from a wild, wild wood; eyes wide shut. Red light falls like a curtain of blood on their black sabbath.

Reader, he married her!

The Shining, dir. Kubrick, 1980
Aurora Orchestra plays Berlioz's Symphonie fantastique—by heart,
Aurora Orchestra, YouTube 2019

Niccolò Paganini, Moto Perpetuo *(1835)*

Gone are the ephemeral lovers' sighs of your *Duetto Amoroso*, those gasping phrases that tugged at the heartstrings eschewed in favour of machine-gun 16ths: 187 measures of the same, frenzied as Pike Bishop at the Battle of Bloody Porch, the circular breathing of your Marfan fingers defying the laws of physics—and time—and by the law of averages it's never stopped ... there's no escape ... someone, somewhere in the world is always playing it: 'Il faut risquer', as every fiddle player knows, battling their demons—*I'll bet a fiddle of gold against your soul, I think I'm better than you*—go on, try it: cut the cop-out cadential chords at 188 and 189 and put it on repeat; keep the software updated; keep the electricity bill paid, the devil at bay, your bid for the future a mash-up of the past

Hellraiser Went Down to Georgia, Motörhead & Primus, RaveDJ, 2019

Frédéric Chopin, Prelude No. 15,
'Raindrop' (1839)

I walk past the end of the white-rosed garden into the field, and beyond, over Round Top Hill, painted with poppies, into the bluebell wood. The sun filters through, and then it's gone, there's a chill in the air and I don't want to be here anymore. The walk back home takes twice as long, unless it's quicker—I can't tell. I sit at the Broadwood piano, unable to play. For every imaginary raindrop there's a spot of human blood, coughed onto ivory. Behind my eyes, the bluebell haze is the colour of tuberculosis. It was Bach who kept you company, along with your lover, as the weather failed you in Majorca; Jagger, in white frock coat who turned to Shelley in Hyde Park, Brian Jones dead in his swimming pool. *Peace, peace! he is not dead, he does not sleep / He has awakened from the dream of life...*
... My fingers begin to move. I manage a little Bach, a little Chopin. A cloud of white butterflies is released, but the crowd doesn't see the thousands that fail to get out of the cardboard boxes.

Bright Star, dir. Campion, 2009

Clara Schumann, Konzertsatz
(1847, unfinished)

Your father names you for the clarity of his purpose, but you have your own; it just won't come as words. Eleven years old and you're rewriting the future, playing from memory, switching the audience on to Bach; somewhere, Glenn Gould is listening in. Franz Lang Lang Liszt can toss his head back like a diva—you don't want to know: *the personality of the musician should be suppressed*. But not the woman, oh no, though you'll find yourself the only one on the faculty of the Frankfurt Konservatorium. You release your husband's *Papillons*, even while your own masterpiece waits in the wings. Eight children, and still you're performing. You walk through the battle zone of Dresden to retrieve the three left behind. The Opera house is burnt to the ground, but there's worse to come; Billy Pilgrim—*unstuck in time*—has already told us, accompanied by Gould, taking us back to Bach yet again, though so little it won't fill an album. Four of your children die and you gather their offspring to your own brood. *So it goes*. And still your Konzertsatz waits for the words it deserves: *If the first full concerto is pedestrian, this fragment inspires that art can be made in those spare moments when the hands are already exhausted from their breadwinning ways.*

for JW

Slaughterhouse-Five, dir. Hill, 1972

Modest Mussorgsky, Pictures at an Exhibition—A Remembrance of Viktor Hartmann *(1874)*

Stunned by the death of your friend, you knock it out in three weeks, walking through his paintings and onward—into the catacombs, *with the dead in a dead language,* but your promenade reappears, and you enter the heroic gate of peerless virtuosity. Ravel has a good stab at it, his remake in colour. Emerson Lake and Palmer crank it up to the max, with the Newcastle City Organ and a modular Moog. We blare it out from our common room window, driving the old masters mad. The promenade goes on. The years assemble paintings into galleries of our own. Every summer we stack the fridge with beers and it's 'Welcome back my friends, to the show that never ends.' The promenade goes on. But Emo begins to suffer from 'writer's cramp' in his right hand; his GX-1 is sold to Hans Zimmer. I break our run of summers, living abroad. When I'm finally home, I open a crate of pictures to find a mess of broken glass, The Queen of the Seas within an inch of her life. Hartmann's own pictures are mostly lost, though Baba Yaga's hut—depicted as a clock—still stands on its chicken feet, the witch of the east careening through your scherzo with her pestle and mortar, grinding our future to dust. Emo's quick-draw hand is painfully slow as he raises a gun to his head in Santa Monica. The promenade is at an end. Our last reunion is in hospital. I write the eulogy, make suggestions for the music. In a few weeks, lockdown.

i.m. KNE, 1944–2016; MTND, 1958–2020

The Wizard of Oz, dir. Fleming, 1939

Richard Wagner,
Götterdämmerung *(1876)*

I place daffodils in the violin-shaped vase that is really a bottle, emptied of some duty-free liqueur from the long weekend when you became *the loveliest girl in Vienna*. It was a treat, not a trick, to take you away from your comfortable Friday night routine. The city knew we had something to celebrate: the bars were strung with cobwebs, a pumpkin on every table; the same story for each of our thirty-five years; three more, since then, when it's been merely Halloween. That day, Mozart's statue was starkly white against autumn leaves. We missed Klimt's kiss in the Belvedere—a long weekend is only so long, though the whole Ring cycle was written to fit. We caught the last five hours—*Twilight*—with champagne between acts. The words, in translation, scrolled past on miniature seatback screens while the music thundered. But twilight, it strikes me now, is not easily understood: it may seem to last forever, but it's little more than the fleeting brush of day against night.

i.m. CEMM, 1959–2017

Inspector Morse, 'Twilight of the Gods', dir. Wise, 1993

Arthur Sullivan, 'The Lost Chord' (1877)

I sit by my father's bed, watching him die—though I don't yet know it. He won't move again, now, though he was longing for a view of the sea—to get away from these claustrophobic woods he used to love. The woods, perhaps, are partly the problem: his imaginings, darker. Today it's the memory that closes in on me, thinking how my mother already knew that view of the sea would be hers alone. Amateur dramatics first brought them together: Gilbert and Sullivan—impossible to mention one without the other. But I think of Sullivan, by his dying brother's bedside, finding a poetic chord elsewhere: *It quieted pain and sorrow, like love overcoming strife; it seemed the harmonious echo from our discordant life.*

i.m. PCEM, 1911–1976; BEM, 1921–1980

Topsy Turvy, dir. Leigh, 2000

Bedřich Smetana, String Quartet No. 1,
'From My Life' (1878)

Antonín Dvořák played viola at the private premiere, in Prague, but you're more likely to have seen Victoria Miskolczy entertaining Robert Redford and his gang. The encryption is unchanged: the same four instruments in intimate debate; the same closed circle of conversation ... until that moment the circuit breaks, the code is cracked, a long, sustained, harmonic eeeeeeeeeeeeeeeeeeee drilling the air straight from the composer's head; his tinnitus—itself the effect of time—unleashed, drilling your own eardrums, the *me* (of *time*), that was once an inaudible, background hum, now morphing to a mundening drone that drives you out of your mind.

Sneakers, dir. Robinson, 1992

*Charles-Marie Widor, Toccata, from
Symphony for Organ No. 5 (1879)*

It plays as the boys spill out of chapel, dreaming of revolt: motorbikes, leathers, girls, (and yes) guns. Our own small act of rebellion was simply to slow it right down — into a grungy calypso with lilting bass, top line overlaid on a languorous synth, everyone on their feet in the sweltering basement of the Olde Worlde Club... We pulled out all the stops, while others pulled bottles of Black Bush from behind the unmanned bar... And yeah, we were trashed after those gigs, but the music was somehow unscathed, the shiny toccata emerging a year later, back up to speed, as you and I walked down the aisle, some of the same faces beaming in the crowd, the music itself now punching the air with a congregated *Yes!*

for TE, MG, CO

If, dir. Anderson, 1968

Camille Saint-Saëns, 'Kangaroos', from
The Carnival of the Animals *(1886)*

It's four hands at play, on two pianos—the reason the kangaroos are at once quietly grazing and bouncing off, a finger-flick levering the triads that gain velocity up the keyboard, before falling away. So purely joyous, so frivolous, you feared for your reputation—*On no account publish this until after my death*—failing to envision your more serious symphony with Farmer Hogget singing to a pig. The modern Olympics kick off, but it's a century later that inflatable kangaroos storm the stage as the Sydney games are announced.

[Splice in verses by Ogden Nash, read by Roger Moore.]

It's a reliable party piece, a mere minute long, but in the 2020 Namadji remix, it's not so much fun; no grace notes to help the roos outpace the blazing grass. The sound, for days—for weeks, months—is the roar of air, sucked into hell. The concert stage is a wasteland of blackened bones.

If I had words to make a day for you, I'd sing you a morning golden and new. I would make this day last for all time; give you a night deep in moonshine.

for TBW

Babe, dir. Noonan, 1995

Claude Debussy, Claire de lune
(1890, rev. 1905)

Fifteen years for the moonlight to be polished. In the water, a waxing reflection of his fame. Verlaine's songbird, forlorn, becomes a nightingale, *magic abroad in the air* ... The ruptured tendon in my left hand leaves the bass notes adrift, and the image blurs—like my tearful vision, *an echo far away.* The song is stolen from a story. *I may be right, I may be wrong.* Enraptured. Or forlorn. *Les grands jets d'eau* play against the Bellagio Hotel. Water, water, every where, as he shifts from his impressionist *Nocturnes* to *La Mer.* Now my arms span the keyboard, the vast harmonic spread of a single chord hauling *La cathedrale engloutie* into the light—the sound so transparent you can hear the bells—even as William Walker, the Winchester Diver, does the same with hammer and pick. You stood at the west end of the nave the night I was there in the choir, processing past the candle-lit tree, my surplice brushing against your skin. Beauty. Beauty is sadness, sadness ... The world goes under. *The streets of town were paved with stars* ... I met you after work outside your office in Berkeley Square. *Our homeward step was just as light as the tap-dancing feet of Astaire.*

Ocean's Eleven, dir. Soderbergh, 2002

Engelbert Humperdink,
Hänsel und Gretel *(1892)*

You follow a breadcrumb trail through the woods, thinking how the son must be cast as a mezzo-soprano. You're a little late to give Siegfried his lesson; by the time you're there, it's not so much Siegfried as a silvered Rick Wakeman rising from Wagner's operating table, grabbing a stein of beer, belching, and pissing on the fire. ('Who's going to follow *him*?' laughs Daltrey-as-Lizst.) The trail doubles back to your more famous faux namesake, crooning his hit cover on a 45-year rollercoaster to Eurovision doom. Suddenly the weather is closing in: the woods are darkening, even as quick snowflakes obliterate the crumbs. Soon the lines are down, the roads all closed. The witch locks up. Wagner's great-great-grandson sits alone in his snowbound studio, giving up on us and writing the TV soundtrack himself. Somewhere, in development, is the Hansel module with *user-customised rules independent from the menu system*, logic switches adding links to the crumbs. Richard Strauss will conduct, Ringo Starr put in a cameo as the Pope. Arnold George Dorsey, post-tuberculosis, keeps 'Penny Lane' off the number one spot, and as war breaks out they won't appoint a German to the Sydney Conservatorium—it's enough to give anyone the hump. Adrian Wagner rubs the Sandman's grit from his eyes and adjusts the mix as a super-bronzed Theseus belts out to Ariadne: *Please release me, let me go ... Release me and let me love again.*

i.m. AW, 1952–2018

Lisztomania, dir. Russell, 1975

*Antonín Dvořák, Symphony No. 9,
'From the New World' (1893)*

The musicassette cover shows me—or someone—crouching above the Grand Canyon, from the days I was in love with America. Today, that's not possible. But as the music plays, I'm tugged back; it's irresistible. A new century is ushered in, full of longing for things left behind. You leave your burrow, blinking into the blinding light.

It was one of these mysterious fairy calls from out the void that suddenly reached Mole in the darkness, making him tingle through and through with its very familiar appeal, even while as yet he could not remember what it was. He stopped dead in his tracks, his nose searching hither and thither in its efforts to recapture the fine filament, the telegraphic current, that had so strongly moved him. A moment, and he had caught it again; and with it this time came recollection in fullest flood.

A boy pushes his bike up the slope of a Cotswold village, sepia toned. The Ashington Colliery Brass Band is at his side, telling us the Old World is still here, though it's not what it used to be. *Hovis.* The day I'm unwell, my father does my paper round, and I never pay him back.

Boy on the Bike, dir. Scott, 1973

Richard Strauss,
Also Sprach Zarathustra *(1896)*

As the monolithic open chord dawns yet again, who can rid their mind of Kubrick's apes, picking a thigh bone from the ground and thinking it into a weapon, drumming the skeletal remains and picturing how a fully-fleshed tapir might likewise be ruthlessly drummed into the dust. It's a small step, but a giant leap, to beat that same rhythm on a fellow ape, thus becoming man. The thigh bone is hurled in slow motion into the air—and onward, into the vast, *eternal recurrence of the same,* the bone a baton, passed to Peckinpah reading Robert Ardrey, who hands it, an iron poker, to Dustin Hoffman as David Sumner, timid mathematician, beating an intruder's head to a pulp. It's a twilight zone of soft-spoken, angry young men—so many one-eyed jacks—but it's the Valkyries who usher in the ultimate carnage, their shrill Wagnerian battle cry pumped out from speakers slung beneath the choppers storming in off the coast, machine guns adding their diegetic rattle as we journey further still into the heart of darkness. Upstream is the slobbery, corrupted übermensch, Colonel Kurtz—the same Brando who cut first Sam, then Stanley from his obsessive pet project, superstardom gone to his straw-filled head—himself now hacked to death, with an innocent buffalo cleavered into pieces live onscreen as ritual accompaniment. It's hard to watch, hard to listen—to a fanfare for the whimpering end of the world.

One-Eyed Jacks, dir. Brando, 1961
2001: A Space Odyssey, dir. Kubrick, 1968
Straw Dogs, dir. Peckinpah, 1971
Apocalypse Now, dir. Coppola, 1979

Edward Elgar, Variations on an Original Theme, 'Enigma' (1899)

'All I wish is, that it may be a lesson to the world, "to let people tell their stories their own way."' —Laurence Sterne

Tell me, Nigel, were you a bit Brahms and Liszt the time you set off fireworks on Elgar's grave, with Yehudi? Did you think you'd cracked the coded secret buried there? Or were you fashioning some controversial portraits of your own? Maybe not portraits, just those small character details that intrigue: your John Lennon shades, the brief beard, the blue and black kaftan; a boy on a white pony, later on a bike, always under an open sky. Let the boy ride free, the camera freely following ... The full theme never appears, like a principal character remaining offstage; your father drinking himself to death in Australia. Your IN-GER-LAND chant reverberates around the Malvern Hills as yet another rocket goes up. Were you channelling the dead man's notorious japes? He's still turning in his grave, his greatest tune hijacked by words not his, used as accompaniment to war and the waving of every union jack. He'd have been happier stony broke: Alice drawing staves, no money for ruled paper; going without fires for a year—Alice, his lifelong love with whom he buried his honours. But what of the other Alice, the Windflower of the concerto? *Aqui está encerrada el alma de* ..... Alice— or maybe Helen; the list goes on. The biggest enigma is what 'Nimrod' is doing at the end of *Australia*. O Baz, what were you *thinking*? And yet, you did it right (Laurence Sterne would be proud), even while getting it so wrong.

Elgar, dir. Russell, 1962
Australia, dir. Luhrmann, 2008

Maurice Ravel, Pavane pour une infante défunte *(1899)*

As if. A Spanish Princess from another age comes to life. Velázquez stares out from his own canvas; his brushstrokes turn to swirling brocade. Critics register a complaint when you perform it yourself, 'unutterably slow', but when others are slower still you've a deadpan quip to hand: It's not a *dead pavanne*. The Princess continues her stately steps like an automaton. Beautiful plumage. Fast forward to the 30s and it's slower still, with lyrics almost warbling to a halt like a failing reel-to-reel. *Dream and watch the shadows come and go, the lamp is low.* It's Gaspard de la nuit who escorts the Princess back into the painterly shadows. Now change the tape to something more upbeat. Tell Cassandra to get her skates on.

                                                          for CA

10, dir. Edwards, 1979

Jean Sibelius, Finlandia *(1899–1900)*

A stone's throw from the beach. Paavo Berglund pulls the Bournemouth Symphony Orchestra through the beat. They're used to it, now, his wayward precision, and you yourself approve: the notes should *swim in the gravy*. In the interval I buy friends underage drinks from the Winter Gardens bar. Paavo's son Pokku and I play violin at school, and on a trip to Germany he blags us seats at the Berlin Philharmonic. At Checkpoint Charlie we have to change currency, then can't find anything to buy. When I return, the wall is gone, rewritten by Roger Waters. The Sony Centre towers over Potsdamer Platz. I can't take it in. I think of your *Finlandia* fail-better rewrites: re-titling, disguising the anti-Russian protest at its core; stripping it back for solo piano; giving it words—and letting others do the same, your music gifted both to stir and still the soul—all the while drinking your way into reclusive decline. 'The Silence of Järvenpää'. I think of the terror—of knowing your best work is behind you—as I sit at the keyboard and stare. *Turn your musical vision into compelling scores for the stage or screen with Sibelius software.* I google Pokku and find he owns a Bordeaux winery. He's written a book: *Wine of the Mind.* Everywhere online there's news of the pandemic. The heatwave soars, and Bournemouth beach is shingled with lager cans, heaving with bodies. Drink again. Drink harder. The sea is like soup.

i.m. PAEB, 1929–2012

for PH

Die Hard 2, dir. Harlin, 1992

Sergei Rachmaninoff,
Piano Concerto No. 2 (1900–01)

What to do, as the century rolls over and Romanticism's dubbed old hat? You pull it tighter, over your ears. Soon will come the charge that such sentiment is treacherous tosh. Hey ho. Another revolution and it's Valentine's Day in the Royal Station Hotel, Carnforth. Opposite is the Station Heritage Centre, where we enjoy a light lunch in the Brief Encounter Refreshment Room. *There's something in my eye.* It's a fleck of the past, as I sit with my father in front of the TV. Why would this possibly work in Winchester, with Richard Burton and Sophia Loren? My father switches it off. Bereft of inspiration, you drive around Beverly Hills in your swanky Ford Exile. *Couples particularly like the location—they rated it 8.8 for a two-person trip. We speak your language!*

Brief Encounter, dir. Lean, 1945

Alma Maria Schindler Mahler Gropius Werfel, 'Einsamer Gang' (2018 [1899])

A secessionist kiss from Gustav Klimt, and so it begins—a lonely walk through a succession of loves, marriages and affairs, barefoot in the rain. At each new encounter she leans in, seductively close, being deaf in one ear from a childhood illness. We all fall for it. She longs to write an opera, even as Kokoschka longs to parade her on his arm at the Teatro La Fenice—goes further, commissioning a full-sized doll in her image, careful that every curve should be perfectly modelled to the memory of his touch. His obsession lingers in our darkest routines. The footfalls we hear behind us mark the path that we follow—along the Fondamenta Contarini to the Casa Mahler, now a hotel—through the gate into her garden; a private paradise. Later, on the Lido, it's her husband's Adagietto that we hear as Visconti persuades us that Aschenbach—longing for a beautiful boy—was a composer, not a writer, but the music is longing for no-one but her, whoever she may be: saint, sinner, or just another misunderstood young girl, a Bernadette. Did the puppet-maker misconstrue, upholstering her lower body with *feathers*? Did Kokoschka, artist, think that an artwork—more than a mere mortal—cannot be rejected, or ignored? Aschenbach's cholera overshadows the disease to which Alma's daughter Manon succumbs, her infantile paralysis the driving force of a sublime concerto 'to the memory of an angel'. 'Lähmungsakkord' is scrawled in the score—and from afar, a Carinthian folksong sounds like lost innocence. Is every affliction blessed by art? Or is it a fate worse than polio, death, to be a *Randfigur*—a muse to the more famous? They were all over her, like flies. *Es ist genug ... lös auf das Band, das allgemählich reißt.* As the sun on the Lido begins to fade, I watch you dive and disappear for so long I begin to panic, thinking the current has dragged you under, away... ... but then you surface, and shake back the water from your hair in a glittering arc. The sparkle seems to hang in the air. Heads turn, as if witnessing a vision.

for FED

The Song of Bernadette, dir. King, 1943 (from the novel by Franz Werfel)
Death in Venice, dir. Visconti, 1971

Sir William Harris, 'Bring Us, O Lord God' (1959)

Barely thirteen, I don't think twice about having tea with a cathedral organist of the nineteenth century. I do think there was toast, as I can hear the whispering scrunch of a knife across the surface. All too soon it's time to go. Your protégé—our choirmaster—drives us back to school. All too soon it's a hearse at the door, first yours, then his; your music the soundtrack; words by John Donne. We mill around in the aisle, afterwards, wondering what to say. We're as lost as Henry Kissinger, Luciano Pavarotti and Sir Elton John—assembling as your prelude ends. Doc H—do they remember you, the sisters in black, from their madrigal practice at Windsor during the war? A full century has passed since you took your place at the organ in St David's, Wales. Words by John Donne; words by Bernie Taupin, David Dimbleby; words of my own, left in the village church pew as I too prepare to play the organ for an English rose. 'And so it ends, with the hearse heading north, under the Scratchwood motorway service station', *to enter into that gate ... where there shall be no darkness nor dazzling, but one equal light; no noise nor silence, but one equal music; no fears nor hopes, but one equal possession; no ends nor beginnings, but one equal eternity ...*

i.m. CCMcW, 1934–2007; PJFJ, 1940–2020

The Funeral of Princess Diana, BBC, 1997

Notes to the Prose Poems
3. 'The Battle of Bloody Porch' is the name given to the dénouement of Sam Peckinpah's film, *The Wild Bunch* (1969).
8. Sullivan's 'The Lost Chord' is based on a poem by Adelaide Anne Procter.
11. Saint-Saëns' theme from his Symphony No. 3 is used in the song 'If I had Words' by Scott Fitzgerald, released in 1978.
12. Debussy's *Claire de lune* is based on Paul Verlaine's poem of the same title. William Walker was a diver who shored up Winchester Cathedral over a period of five years, 1906–1911. 'A Nightingale Sang in Berkeley Square' was written by Manning Sherwin, with lyrics by Eric Maschwitz. The title was taken from a story in Michael Arlen's 1923 collection, *These Charming People*.
13. Engelbert Humperdinck, aka Arnold 'Gerry' Dorsey, came 25th out of 26 in the Eurovision Song Contest, 2012. His hit 'Release Me' had spent 56 weeks in the top 50, 1967–8. He is still touring. Paul Munden and Kit Monkman were due to work with Adrian Wagner on television music in 1991. Their new film, *The Darkroom*, is currently in pre-production.
14. The central quotation is from Kenneth Grahame's *The Wind in the Willows* (1908). Ridley Scott's 1973 Hovis advert was remastered and screened again in 2019.
17. Ravel's Pavane was adapted as a popular song by Peter DeRose and Bert Shefter, with lyrics by Mitchell Parish. Ravel's piano suite *Gaspard de la nuit* (1909) is based on the prose poem collection by Aloysius Bertrand. Cassandra Atherton is (or was) a keen skater.
18. Roger Waters staged a version of Pink Floyd's *The Wall* in Berlin on 21 July 1990. Paul Hetherington and Bruce Willis have never been seen in the same room.
19. Rachmaninoff left Russia after the revolution, finally settling in Beverly Hills in 1942.
20. Visconti's *Death in Venice* is based on Thomas Mann's novel of the same name. Alban Berg dedicated his violin concerto (codedly) to Manon Gropius. It makes use of Bach's chorale, 'Es ist genug'.
21. William Harris was appointed as assistant organist at St David's, Wales, in 1897, aged 14. Clement McWilliam, for several years sub-organist at Winchester Cathedral, was assistant to William Harris at the Royal Chapel, Windsor, 1959.

The Persistence of Vision

JEN WEBB

'We grope our way, largely in the dark, about our respective caves. The world, to a large extent, is a vision of our own creation.'

—*Leif Finkel*

'From the first moment, I handled my lens with a tender ardour, and it has become to me as a living thing, with voice and memory and creative vigour.'

—*Julia Margaret Cameron*

L'Arrivée d'un train	83
Alchemy	84
Original Sin	85
Through a Glass, Darkly	86
The Lesson	87
Winter in Lyon	88
The Image and the Eye	89
The Grammar of Perception	90
Arrested Gesture	91
The Birth of Cinema	92
The New Immortals	93
The Frame of the Nineteenth Century	94
Shadow Play	95
In the Eye of the Machine	96
The Myth of Cinema	97
My Mother Myself	98
Promio in Chicago	99
What Happened in 1869	100
The Inventors	101
Intimations of Mortality	102
The Transit of Venus	103

L'Arrivée d'un train

It's that film we've all seen of a train approaching Lyon Station. Backdrop of hill and clouded sky, foreground of well-dressed crowd who turn their faces to watch the train arrive, turn again as in a tennis match to see it pass. Travellers spill down the steps, and shift themselves between passers-by and porters hauling bags. Women in exuberant skirts rush to embrace friends, to hoist their kids. Sharp fellows saunter past, as glossy as the train itself, children and women and men all black-and-white and shades of grey. A man I'd invite home stares into the lens then pivots out of sight.

Deep focus, single shot, moving image mistaken for reality. IMBD rating: one star.

Not quite the first-ever film, *L'Arrivée d'un train à La Ciotat* (1896) has a listing on IMDB. Director/producer Auguste Lumière and Louis Lumière; starring Madeleine Koehler and Marcel Koehler.

Alchemy

'In the end, what is certain is perhaps the only factor that really matters in a work of art. This image of a leaf ... arrests our attention as much today as it has done for at least a century and a half.' —Larry J Schaaf

They called it science but she knew it to be art. Knew it by the demands it made on her; the finished work she pictured on the screen in her mind; the slow concentration needed to salt silver over heavy rag, measure out time in micrograms over the grain of the page, add emulsion, dry her sheets in shadow. It takes time, she told her doubtful dad, and light, and an eye to see art in the everyday. It takes a steady hand. She cuts a leaf still green, to die in silver long before its time. Leaf looks up into the sun, and sun returns its gaze, and the silver paper opens up to sun and shadow and when she lifts the page, there it is, a photo-graph, a poem written in light; and there she is, making a mark, crafting a world where the ordinary is seen in all its being, suddenly arcane.

Sarah Anne Bright (Bristol UK, 1793–1866), thought to be the first woman photographer, remained unknown, her works attributed to one or other man until, in 2015, art historian Larry Schaaf identified her initials on a photogram she had produced of a leaf, possibly as early as 1805, more probably 1839.

Original Sin

'To try to catch transient reflected images is not merely something that is impossible, but ... the very desire to do so is blasphemy. Man is created in the image of God and God's image cannot be captured by any human machine.'
—*The Leipzig City Advertiser*

It leaches slowly into the human soul, they tell us; comes dressed in the disguise of science. Stomp on it, the preacher insists, as one would stomp a snail. Crush it before you find yourself caught, like Laocoön and his sons, no exit sign to mark the spot, no uniformed usher lighting a narrow path toward the door. We have heard the sermons, read the tracts, but still: to *capture the image of God*, to collect in a net *transient reflected images of the divine*— what a perfect blasphemy that would be! Reach me my camera; show me this new sin of seeing.

Through a Glass, Darkly

Fuck the critics. I know what I know and I will write in light as my eyes insist. 'It may amuse you, Mother', said my girl, handing me my first camera, and I learned the delights of the darkroom, of wet collodion, glass plates. Learned my passion for the human form, the nobility a lens can confer. *Out of focus* said the critics, condemning me along with my work. *Slovenly manipulation; a want of precision.* But I dissent; it's only me who transforms milkmaid to Madonna, builds beauty on an armature of the ordinary. Like a true artist. *Stand there*, I command my subjects; and they stand, and become patterns of eternity.

Julia Margaret Cameron (Calcutta, London, 1815–1879) innovated portrait photography, using a sliding-box camera and glass plates. Famously, she photographed an already bald and bearded Charles Darwin in 1868.

The Lesson

Now I am five you have shown me your new trick. A disc that bears a horse, frozen mid-canter, and a man in motion. A smaller disc you set above the first, and then—*Watch*, you say, and spin the two, and man falls from horse, and rises, and falls again, falling and flying between horse and the unforgiving edge until I too fall, all vertigo, and you pack the toy away. I am folded on the floor, watching you watch the world as it turns. *This is not a trick*, you say; we are always in motion. I plot the passage of shadow across floor, of planets across sky. Now I am grown I can see that we are falling and rising and falling again, suspended between earth and sky by a force we cannot comprehend.

Phénakisticope (1833) [from Ancient Greek phenakistés ('cheat, imposter') + skopéo ('inspect, look into, consider'). Designed by Joseph Plateau (1801–1833).

Winter in Lyon

So now we can de-oldify history, the people of Lyon fling their snowballs and the twentieth century adds a soundtrack, honky-tonk from a tack piano borrowed from some western bar, and their clothes are crisp again, the black so very black, the snow bleaching Louis' film the way snow bleaches everything, even you, when for a moment you are blind. A cyclist pedals through the mêlée but speed is no solution and the snowballs burst above him like stars, like shells, a shatter of light and he struggles to his feet, struggles to his bike, pedals in haste back the way he came. Here's your tender heart: you see his hat neglected on the road and try to snatch it, chase him down, restore it with regrets, but *No*, says Louis, *we'll sort it out tomorrow.*

Bataille de boules de neige (1896), director Louis Lumière; filmed, developed and projected on a *cinématographe*, 35mm format, aspect ratio 1.33:1. No IMDB rating.

The Image and the Eye

The eyes do in fact follow you about the room. They sense the edges of your skin, bore through to what you are only now beginning to apprehend: that you are sliding oblivious into history. Now you notice the shadow of your skin, and that it won't come off, not even with soap and scrubbing. The photograph is becoming more you than you know yourself to be. Late at night she hears you murmur that you are being left behind.

EH Gombrich's *The Image and the Eye* (1994) recounts the psychology of seeing, tricks of perspective, and the relationship between the seen and the lived world that were imposed on populations as part of the 19th century's determination to understand and exploit visuality.

The Duty of the Camera

'Photography must return to its proper duty which consists in being a servant to the sciences and the arts.'
—Charles Baudelaire

You see only what can be seen, given the limits of the human eye, given the blind spot that blurs the scenery so you miss the man coming too rapidly toward you, can't catch the number plate of that car you almost hit. You see what you see but your eye is never still, a blur in the print even when your body, propped against the chair, is perfectly composed. This new machine, undistracted, looks across the street with a gaze cool and interested as a swan. It captures every breath, corrects all you have always got wrong: the way a shoulder curves from the spine, how a horse canters in three beat bars. Sees the baby banging his spoon on the bowl, a train drawing in to a station. Every movement a miracle.

Arrested Gesture

'How to imagine not only a new art or architecture, but a new self or subject adequate to them? ' —Hal Foster

The fall and fold of his greatcoat, its lines drawing the eye out and across the picture plane, his cravat shimmering with light that struggles to be seen. Everything is moving but the man; still the photographer enjoins him to *sit still, will you?* and his eyes shift as his neck stiffens, shoulders groan. He will have proof that he was in the world, his brief transit captured in permanent form. A century on, his granddaughter will pause while turning stiff pages in the album that has been propped on the piano all her life, and gaze at him, a stranger in a strange land.

The Birth of Cinema

Deranged midwife waves magic wand among overgrown cabbages that fill the garden, paleolithic roses hiding squalling babies that she lifts, mad grin in place, displays and then oops drops them, and pirouettes away. Their tiny feet, aggrieved, kick at heartless air; their silent shrieks mere background. Some fairy; some story; but *Birth is always cruel*, says mother, and babies far less content than your Anne Geddes snaps suggest. And then—is that a coke can on her head? Is the third baby really dead?

Alice Guy-Blaché (1873–1968), *La Fée aux Choux* (*The Cabbage Fairy*), 1896. This, considered the world's first narrative film, leans heavily on the logic of fairytale. For a 21st-century eye, it's hard on the kids; for 19th-century critics, it was a 'chaste fiction of children born under the cabbages'.

The New Immortals

'Man has, as it were, become a kind of prosthetic God. When he puts on all his auxiliary organs he is truly magnificent; but those organs have not grown on to him and they still give him much trouble at times.' —Sigmund Freud

When you speak, all sound fails. Colours fade from the screen. There's just your mouth moving out of sync, your eyes frozen, closed. And then the world jerks ahead and you're tap dancing toward me at 16 frames per second, jittering from step to step, dodging some kid who runs across the scene, chasing a ball between time zones, and he's gone before the crazy guy cranking the wooden box camera can shout. The grip rolls the tripod off stage; the director checks his watch; someone hands out cups of tea. You stand, hand on hip, cigarillo at your lips, waiting for the next scene.

The Frame of the Nineteenth Century

'The age of dialectic logic is the age of photography and film or, if you like, the frame of the nineteenth century.'—Paul Virili

Forget Kepler; he's so seventeenth century; and anyway his machine is so passé. Also forget Alhazen's optics, which no one reads anymore; and Mozi's darkened room; forget those cavemen and their thaumatropes carved out of bone. We are the nineteenth century, and we're *here!* and *here!* and *now!* We are the machines of the visible, the logic of motion and change. A mouse runs at twelve frames per second across a room. A woman gathers her skirts, leapfrogs a milking stool. Finally we can render the things we could not see. We have built a science of seeing. We are writing the evidence of someone else's eyes.

Shadow Play

'If "reality" is truly the "lost object of our desires", then perhaps "a little forgetting allows the past to inform but not overwhelm the present".' —Adrian Parr

The film hiccups and he is stranded on screen, black-and-white boho, self-consciously cool. Cracking celluloid dissolves his shoulder into a scatter of light; his hand as it sweeps back his hair is a muddied blur. Someone is fiddling with the projector; someone is lighting a cigarette; and at the back of the room two kids are learning the epistemology of love. Years later, friends again after messy affairs and marriages and disappointing careers, they will recall over cognac how their early passion faded into chiaroscuro, the smoke from phantom cigarettes, that man on screen whose name they can't recall.

In the Eye of the Machine

'Photographs are not so much an instrument of memory as an invention of it or a replacement.' —Susan Sontag

It warms up slowly, the steam coughing and stretching as it makes its way through the coils. You grind the beans, twist the filter into place, press the little button on the left, and gold spills into the cup and crema glibbers across its top. Now we're slipping into overdrive, every wire humming, living our best fucking lives. Take me there, he murmurs in your ear, barely audible over the hum and clack, the whistle and whine of all these seeing machines. But where are you, in fact? Is this memory, or some kind of ghost? Last week I snapped you on my 35mil SLR, but later when I twisted my loupe into place to eyeball the proof sheet there was no image. Yet I saw you; lifting your cup, breathing in the drift of deep roast beans. Here from the future I see you still. Struggling to breathe.

The Myth of Cinema

We meet in that space you always call the River of Time, wearing a mirrored shawl that someone brought you from India. It shows dark grey on the plate, flickers of light animating the screen. It's fine enough to draw through a wedding ring, if you had a wedding ring, if I had such a thing. When you look at me, you say, all you see is a halo of light. Though halo is not what you mean. I am yearning for the touch of skin, for the feel of yours or someone's breath against my hand, against my face. You are adrift. You are drifting away from yourself, and from me, and soon there will be only rainbow scattered across the screen, a hint of some small interruption of time, of light.

Einstein's 'River of Time' does not flow in a linear fashion, but meanders. Time, and light, are both waves and particles, so that the present is always here, and also far away. 'People like us, who believe in physics, know that the distinction between the past, present and future is only a stubbornly persistent illusion' (Einstein 1955).

My Mother Myself

A girl and another girl, a woman in a mirror, a secret *mise-en-scène*. A woman in a dark room, watching line form on page. She has dressed her daughters, trained them in the posing of passion, the freezing of smile. She sets guncotton and ether over glass to capture their gestures; arranges the fall of arm, the coil of hair. A girl looks out from a mirror, pre-Pre-Raphaelite; a girl clutches a curtain under the force of some unspoken urge. Two sisters stretch bare-legged, becoming women, under the sun, under their mother's eye.

Lady Clementina Hawarden (1822–1865) made albumen prints from wet-collodion negatives, and from the late 1850s to the mid-1860s photographed her adolescent daughters in what are usually described as 'sensual poses'.

Promio in Chicago

And it's *The first movie ever shot in the Windy City. Featuring you'll be astounded to hear police on parade*, and they're Keystone Cops with Thomson & Thompson moustache, marching obliquely past. In Geneva it's bighorn sheep and skullcapped boys and an old man who plays an alphorn, silently. Heading south, you see two men paddle a traghetto while vaporetti power past; and then it's the Jaffa Gate where passersby peer into the lens. The camera is crossing the globe. Everywhere, ordinary people are doing ordinary things, astoundingly. You stand on the corner of Madison and State, stand on the Rialto, stand at the Wall; filming 40-second films for Instagram; waiting for posterity to call.

Alexandre Promio (1868–1926), trained and employed by the Lumière brothers, travelled widely during 1896–97, making the first film ever in Chicago, using the first ever moving camera in Venice, filming the first ever Swedish newsreel, and spreading the gospel of the cinématographe worldwide.

What Happened in 1869?

A seething world: everywhere ideas are on the march. And it's war, and politics, and art, the banning of the Klan, there's new music and Maori Wars, shoguns are fading and everywhere women are being seen. We learn to make margarine, invent the periodic table, monarchs rise and fall and gold makes fools of men. Rasputin is born; Roget dies. We too are born into this trembling world, where we jerk on out of sync with the shot, then dying we judder toward the grave. You are propped on the good couch, holding your dead child, proving for someone that she, and you, were here.

According to Robert Bishop McLaughlin of Syracuse University (1989), 'The contemporary world's casual attitude toward photography has belied its significant capacity to define, enrich, and alter every aspect of human life.' Before the 19th century, one had to take another's word for what had happened.

The Inventors

'A casual reading of the history of film suggests that it was a logical sequence of development. But, like all else in the history of science, "it leapt about, split, converged, diverged, got into jams and corners". It regularly succeeded, regularly failed.'
—Paul Clee

They make, and pull apart, and reassemble; schoolboys tormenting flies, a teacher marking children's work. Ancient patterns, and new, are suddenly seen, as when an artist observes a table lamp, its flutter of shadows and light, how it reflects in, and off mirrors, almost like motion. You walk slowly across a room, observing every step. You walk slowly across a room, recording the shift of muscle and meat, how bones move smoothly through their cycle. If this, then that. Make a wheel of life; show a mouse pretending to be a cat, a cat pretending to be a man. This might be the change that is as good as a holiday, a picture worth a thousand words.

Intimations of Mortality

The light reflecting off the cracked surface of the canal, scattered against the daubed walls of our buildings. The streets shift improbably under our feet. Subtle but certain, that reminder that all we have is fleeting. We pose before the canal, arm in arm, breathing, and later collect the cards from the man who watched us, calling instructions from under the cape. We will post the cards back home, our tiny gesture to the past. You tell me this will never change, even as buildings slide under the sea, as even our photos crumple and blur, and silence overlays your lovely face where you pose, downcast eyes, hands in lap.

Charles Baudelaire, 'The Painter of Modern Life', saw modernity as being 'the ephemeral, the fugitive, the contingent', though it also constituted 'one half of art'. This sets up a tension and dissatisfaction that is not easily resolved.

The Transit of Venus

Move across the window; your shadow falls between the sun and the cat who sleeps among roses you scattered to brighten the day, and we dance across their petals till I become Venus, flying against the grain. You are manning the camera, and each shot measures the distance between me and tomorrow. Dearest, we are rich in roses but not in time, I say. But you claim the order in uncertainty, and among the algorithms you shoo my doubt away. Turn your face to the future, pass the popcorn, press play.

The 1874 Transit of Venus galvanised scientists and photographers; French astronomer Pierre Janssen travelled to Japan with his 'photographic revolver' to take a series of photos of the 1874 transit, and other photographers scattered across the globe, hoping to secure the perfect shot. According to John Lankford ('Photography and the 19th-Century Transits of Venus', 1987), they failed.

Individual Poet Statements

CASSANDRA ATHERTON

Tim Barringer argues, 'the Pre-Raphaelites aimed to revive aspects from before the time of Raphael (1483–1520), in order to reform British painting ... the 'PRB' label was a gesture of defiance [and] signalled the rejection of centuries of accumulated tradition which revered Raphael and ... Michelangelo (1999: 7). In the 20th and 21st centuries, many people first encounter Pre-Raphaelite art online or in mass-produced prints, in frames, on t-shirts, jewellery or handbags. This seems vaguely fitting as the art world has never fully embraced the Pre-Raphaelites. William Cook argues this is partly because 'Pre-Raphaelite art was collected by industrialists, new money not old—snobbery kept it out of fashion' (2012: n.p.).

Interestingly, one of the most famous collectors of Pre-Raphaelite art today is Sir Andrew Lloyd Webber, whose music has attracted similar criticisms tied to elitism. Indeed, when Elizabeth Prettejohn argues Pre-Raphaelite art is 'perennially popular with wider audiences' (2012: 7), she demonstrates that in the world of art, 'popular' is often a pejorative term. While some curators may argue that this is no longer the case with the Pre-Raphaelites, we only have to look at Tate Britain in London, which houses many of the famous Pre-Raphaelite paintings, to see the enduring prejudice. While the paintings could be said to be a loose presentation of how they might have been displayed in Victorian houses, the multitude of paintings are cramped in one room, vying for wall space. Many of the JMW Turner paintings, by contrast, are exhibited one painting to a wall. The majority of visitors stand in the 'Pre-Raphaelite room', often queueing to take photos of themselves next to their favourite artworks—another way they are stigmatised as having a popular rather than serious appreciation of art.

This chapbook celebrates the enduring appeal and popularity of Pre-Raphaelite art in the 21st century and aims to capture the way the paintings continue to speak to the quotidian experience, even in (or, in part, because of) their hyper-realism. It also acknowledges the ways in which prose poetry intersects with many of these concerns, where prose poetry is expressed in humble sentences and paragraphs, rather than lines and stanzas.

The Pre-Raphaelite Brotherhood was a boys' club, with Dante Gabriel Rossetti's favourite description of the acronym being identified as 'Penis Rather Better'. Furthermore, the original members—John Everett Millais, William Holman Hunt and Rossetti—trawled the streets for 'stunners'—stunning women to be their models, muses and often lovers. Jan Marsh argues, 'Women are important in the Pre-Raphaelite movement. But while their faces are seen everywhere—in oil paintings, watercolours, drawings—their voices are never heard' (1985: 1). In 2018, for International Women's Day, I was asked how I would like to be photographed. I wanted to revisit Millais' painting of Elizabeth Siddall as Ophelia. Instead of dying, I floated in a lake in a red ballgown, reading a book of women's poetry. It was a small attempt at recasting the moment in both literature and art in a feminist frame.

The prose poems in this chapbook are ekphrastic. The trap of ekphrasis is to produce a flat description that does nothing more than describe the work of art; instead ekphrastic writing should shift or transform a work or works of art in an original way. However, in understanding the importance of this transformation, I often feel overwhelmed by the visual power of Pre-Raphaelite paintings. This is something akin to Peter Wagner's description of ekphrasis as having 'a Janus face: as a form of mimesis, it stages a paradoxical performance, promising to give voice to the allegedly silent image even while attempting to overcome the power of the image by transforming and inscribing it' (Wagner 1996: 13). Paul Hetherington and I co-edited an ekphrastic issue of *Cordite Poetry Review* in 2017 and in discussing Wagner's quotation, he offered me the best piece of advice I have had on composing an ekphrastic work: if the painting could talk, what would it tell you?

Nikki Santilli has argued that, historically, the French prose poem has been closely identified with the art book. This is because concise texts accompany and often imitate visual images. More specifically, prose poetry could be considered the perfect form for ekphrasis because it often appears, visually, as a rectangle hanging on a page. In this way, it mimics a painting hanging on the wall of a gallery. In this chapbook, I have given each of my ekphrastic Pre-Raphaelite prose poems a page of their own, liberating them from the cramped confines in some galleries. But I have added another rectangle to the frame—that of the iPhone or screen.

Post-Raphaelite references the challenges faced by art galleries and museums during COVID-19. In Melbourne, stage four lockdown continued for four months (at the time of writing) with everything except essential services shut down. It celebrates the posting of art on social media for the way it can unite broad communities and encourage the reciprocal posting of responses in comment sections. It celebrates art and poetry for all people, everywhere.

Works Cited

Atherton, C and Hetherington, P 2017 'Cordite Ekphrastic', *Cordite Poetry Review*, 57 (1), http://cordite.org.au/content/poetry/ekphrastic/

Barringer, T 1998 *Reading the Pre-Raphaelites*, London: Weidenfeld and Nicolson

Cook, W 2012 'At Home with the Pre-Raphaelites', *The Spectator*, 15 September

Marsh, J 1985 *The Pre-Raphaelite Sisterhood*, New York, NY: St Martins Press

Prettejohn, E (ed) 2012 *The Cambridge Companion to The Pre-Raphaelites*, Cambridge: Cambridge University Press

Wagner P (ed) 1996 *Icons-Text-Iconotexts: Essays on Ekphrasis and Intermediality*, New York, NY: de Gruyter

PAUL HETHERINGTON

Many brilliant and diverse novels were written in the 19th century, not only in English but in a wide variety of countries. Individual novels from the period are so well-known that one has only to think of some of them—*Wuthering Heights* is an excellent example—to summon a powerful set of characters and incidents that, in certain circumstances, may seem almost as real—or even more real—than events in one's own life.

The prose poetry sequence, *The Novel Reader*, explores how quotations from various 19th-century novels incorporated within contemporary prose poetry may be constructed as a highly suggestive framework for the prose poems' contemporary concerns. In particular, *The Novel Reader* explores themes and motifs already familiar from many 19th-century novels★—most obviously, the nature of problematic relationships between men and women in societies where women are not permitted an equal place and gender stereotyping is the norm.

The Novel Reader updates these concerns while showing their continuing relevance in the 21st century and, in doing so, each of the sequence's individual prose poems is constructed as a kind of dialogue with a particular 19th-century work. To give one example, the first prose poem in the sequence quotes from Charles Dickens' *Little Dorrit* to help it establish its themes of confinement and privation.

However, the preoccupations of these prose poems are never entirely congruent with the preoccupations of the novels they quote from. As a result, while each of the 19th-century quotations to a significant extent complements and, as it were, enlarges the contemporary prose poems they inhabit, they also represent something of a counter-narrative that inflects or challenges the prose poems' contemporary contexts and ideas. As Marko Juvan puts it, '[c]ertain ... allusion markers, metonymically call up a referential text, making the reader simultaneously activate two textual worlds' (2008: 70).

Thus, adopting an explicit and conscious intertextuality as a prose-poetic technique allows *The Novel Reader* to pay homage to and recontextualise existing works while also modifying these works and their implications. The sequence contains at least two kinds of suggestiveness—that which derives from the 19th-century quotations and their associations, and contemporary ideas and contexts.

This meshing of old and new in *The Novel Reader* is an opportunity to consider how literary texts are continually being modified by every reader and how the act of reading creates its own 'realities'. Norman N Holland comments that a literary work 'finds its fulfillment ... when a reader gives it life by re-creating the work in his [or her] own mind. The text as such almost vanishes in the astonishing variability of different readers' re-creation of it' (2011: 13). This prose poetry sequence also examines some of the ways in which texts from a markedly different historical period retain the sometimes surprising capacity to speak persuasively to readers about contemporary issues.

Works Cited

Holland, NN 2011 *The Nature of Literary Response: Five Readers Reading*, New Brunswick, NJ: Transaction

Juvan, M 2008 *History and Poetics of Intertextuality* (trans T Pogacar), West Lafayette, IN: Purdue University Press

* The exception is that volume one of *The Wings of the Dove* was published in 1902, but the novel is based on the 19th-century life of Minny Temple.

PAUL MUNDEN

When we encounter 19th-century music today it is invariably through an interpretation; we don't face the 'original' as we can with visual works of art. True, the curation/context of those originals might affect our encounter, but the connection is undoubtedly more direct; with music, interpretation is all; even if we deal directly with the original score, an imaginative leap is required, more than with literature. Thomas Edison's phonograph, invented in 1877 was a breakthrough, but presented more distortion than original music, and the remarkable Ampico (American Piano Company) piano roll, that enabled Rachmaninoff to make faithful reproductions of his own performances of his works (1991), only became available in 1916 (preceded by the German Welte Mignon version in 1904).

The 'historically informed performance' movement has attempted to close the interpretation gap, but remains highly speculative—and indeed divorced from other performative lines of connection. Ultimately, it's impossible to achieve historical 'accuracy', as that would necessitate performers acquiring an entirely 19th-century sensibility. And what would actually be the point? As Tom Service (2020) has said, music has to be remade as urgently as possible, and I take 'urgency' to imply a direct connection with the *present* as well as the past. It is this principle that has driven my particular dual focus within these poems, along with other aspects of Romanticism: the 'emphasis ... on strangeness' and 'boundlessness'; its aspiration 'to transcend immediate times or occasions, to seize eternity, to reach back into the past and forward into the future' (Grout 1973: 539); and 'the accent on the individual' (543). Significantly, as Grout states: 'The [19th-century] arts themselves tend to merge; poetry, for example, aims to acquire the qualities of music, and music the characteristics of poetry' (540).

In the 19th century, program music—which associates itself with 'poetic, descriptive, or even narrative subject matter' (ibid: 540)—comes into its own. This capacity to speak of other elements is both intriguing and imprecise. It's possible, for instance, to 'misread' Debussy's 'faun'* for a 'fawn' and for the music still to 'work' (in light of which it's less than absurd that Sibelius's *Finlandia* was the national anthem of Biafra). But with the notion of 'program' begins music's association with film, which forms another thematic and structural element within my poems. Some 19th-century composers wrote for the cinema (Saint-Saëns was one of the first; others such as Erich Korngold were more prolific), and the further use of 'Romantic' musical soundtracks has been vast. It wasn't difficult to identify films relating to each of the musical compositions on which my poems are based.

The music/film/poetry exchange is further complicated by the turbulent oppositions that characterise 19th-century art. Lawrence Kramer highlights 'dialectical reversals' that lead to 'heightenings of subjective intensity ... with advances in insight or self-possession, but more often with mental pain' (1990: 73). The contrast of style within Chopin's Prelude in A Minor (as analysed by Kramer), between the melody in the right hand and the harmony of the left, is one such dialectic, and relates interestingly to the contrasts typical of Keith Emerson's 20th-century compositions and arrangements. His version of Aaron Copland's *Fanfare for the Common Man* (1977), for instance, pitches Copland's melody against a driving rock bass line (vertical contrast) and inserts an entirely improvised central section (horizontal contrast), all of which Copland himself approved. These are the type of tactics that my poems employ, with both the dark and lighter aspects of life in the mix.

Works Cited

Emerson, K 1977 *Works, Volume 1* (LP), Los Angeles, CA: Atlantic Records

Grout, DJ 1973 *A History of Western Music* (rev. edn), London: JM Dent & Sons

Kramer, L 1990 *Music as Cultural Practice, 1800–1900*, Berkeley, CA: University of California Press

Lloyd, R 2005, *Mallarmé: The Poet and His Circle*, Ithaca, NY: Cornell University Press

Rachmaninov, S 1991 *Rachmaninov plays Rachmaninov: The Ampico Piano Recordings 1919-29* (CD), London: Decca

Service, T 2020 *The Listening Service* (broadcast/podcast), London: BBC

Valéry, P 1972 *Collected Works of Paul Valéry*, Volume 8 (trans M Cowley and JR Lawler), London: Routledge & Kegan Paul

---

* Claude Debussy's *Prélude à l'après-midi d'un faune* (1894) is based on a poem by Stéphane Mallarmé, who was initially hostile; according to Paul Valery, 'He believed that his own music was sufficient, and that even with the best intentions in the world, it was a veritable crime as far as poetry was concerned to juxtapose poetry and music, even if it were the finest music there is' (Valéry 1972: 263). He changed his mind, however, having attended the premiere, writing to Debussy: 'I've just left the concert and am deeply moved: what a marvel! your illustration of "The Afternoon of a Faun" offers no dissonance with my text, except that it goes further, truly, in nostalgia and light, with finesse, uneasiness, and richness' (in Lloyd 2005: 154).

JEN WEBB

Optical devices have been around from at least the Late Paleolithic era, with its bone thaumatropes and animated cave paintings, its 'pre-echoes' of cinema (Azéma and Rivère 2012). The Chinese philosopher Mozi (470–390 BCE) explained the principles of the pinhole camera (Zhang 2020); and the tenth-century Muslim scholar Al-Basri (Alhazen) refined concepts of the camera obscura (Tbakhi and Amr 2007). But the images produced up to the 19th century were ephemeral: not till Wedgwood's photogram, Niépe's heliographic, Daguerre's process, and Talbot's calotype, had Europeans cracked the problem of fixing still images.

'Philosophical toys'—thaumatrope, praxinoscope, zoetrope et al—provided the means to explore depth and movement, time and space (Wade 2004), exploiting the persistence of vision. Muybridge showed how to study the movement of people and animals; and Janssen's astronomical revolver added the ability to trace the movement of celestial objects. Next, of course, came film cameras, and then we were on the doorstep of the age of cinematography.

Film histories focus on the contributions of European men, but film and photography emerged also across Asia, the Middle East and the Americas; and women were key agents right from the start, their photographs interrupting the myth of female passivity, presenting women confident in their skin, performing new ways of being human (Raymond 2017). Early films were remarkably quotidian in content—everyday people, marvellously doing everyday things—but women infused this new form with imagination and narrative. Their contributions to the wonders of the 19th century still murmur in my ears.

Works Cited

Azéma, M and Rivère, F 2012 'Animation in Palaeolithic art: A Pre-echo of Cinema', *Antiquity* 86 (332), 316–24

Raymond, C 2017 *Women Photographers and Feminist Aesthetics*, London: Routledge

Tbakhi, A and Amr, SS 2007 'Ibn Al-Haytham: Father of Modern Optics', *Annals of Saudi Medicine* 27 (6), 464–67

Wade, NJ 2004 'Philosophical Instruments and Toys: Optical Devices Extending the Art of Seeing', *Journal of the History of the Neurosciences* 13 (1), 102–24

Zhang, Y 2020 'The Historical Significance of Mohist Scientific Thought', *Journal of Scientific and Social Research* 2 (2), 62–65

ABOUT THE POETS

CASSANDRA ATHERTON is an award-winning writer and scholar of prose poetry. She was a Visiting Scholar in English at Harvard University and a Visiting Fellow in Literature at Sophia University, Tokyo. Her most recent books of prose poetry are *Leftovers* (2020) and *Fugitive Letters* (2020). She is currently working on a book of prose poetry on the atomic bomb, with funding from the Australia Council. Cassandra co-wrote *Prose Poetry: An Introduction* (2020) and co-edited *The Anthology of Australian Prose Poetry* (2020) with Paul Hetherington. She is a commissioning editor for *Westerly* magazine and series editor for *Spineless Wonders*.

PAUL HETHERINGTON is a distinguished poet who has published numerous full-length poetry and prose poetry collections and has won or been nominated for more than thirty national and international awards and competitions. He is Professor of Writing in the Faculty of Arts and Design at the University of Canberra, head of the International Poetry Studies Institute (IPSI) and joint founding editor of the international online journal *Axon: Creative Explorations*. He founded the International Prose Poetry Group in 2014. He is co-author of a scholarly study of the prose poem for Princeton University Press (2020), and co-editor of the *Anthology of Australian Prose Poetry* (2020).

PAUL MUNDEN is a poet, editor and screenwriter living in North Yorkshire. He has published five poetry collections, most recently *Chromatic* (UWA Publishing, 2017). He was director of Poetry on the Move, 2015–2017, and director of the UK's National Association of Writers in Education, 1994–2018. He has worked as conference poet for the British Council, reader for Stanley Kubrick, and is the current poetry editor of *Westerly* magazine. He is a Royal

Literary Fund Fellow at the University of Leeds, and an Adjunct Associate Professor at the University of Canberra. He is co-editor with Alvin Pang and Shane Strange of *No News: 90 Poets Reflect on a Unique BBC Newscast* (Recent Work Press, 2020).

JEN WEBB is Dean, Graduate Research, and Distinguished Professor of Creative Practice at the University of Canberra. The ACT editor of Australian Book Review's *States of Poetry* anthology, co-editor of the bilingual anthology *Open Windows: Contemporary Australian Poetry*, the literary journal *Meniscus*, and the scholarly journal *Axon: Creative Explorations*, she is also author of several poetry collections and artist books. Her most recent poetry collection is *Moving Targets* (Recent Work Press, 2018).

IPSI: International Poetry Studies Institute

The International Poetry Studies Institute (IPSI) is part of the Centre for Creative and Cultural Research, Faculty of Arts and Design, University of Canberra. IPSI conducts research related to poetry, and publishes and promulgates the outcomes of this research internationally. The institute also publishes poetry and interviews with poets, as well as related material, from around the world. Publication of such material takes place in IPSI's online journal *Axon: Creative Explorations* (www.axonjournal.com.au) and through other publishing vehicles, such as Axon Elements. IPSI's goals include working—collaboratively, where possible—for the appreciation and understanding of poetry, poetic language and the cultural and social significance of poetry. The institute also organises symposia, seminars, readings and other poetry related activities and events.

CCCR: Centre for Creative and Cultural Research

The Centre for Creative and Cultural Research (CCCR) is IPSI's umbrella organisation and brings together staff, adjuncts, research students and visiting fellows who work on key challenges within the cultural sector and creative field. A central feature of its research concerns the effects of digitisation and globalisation on cultural producers, whether individuals, communities or organisations.

www.ingramcontent.com/pod-product-compliance
Lightning Source LLC
Chambersburg PA
CBHW021955290426
44108CB00012B/1084